LUSTRE
for
China Painters and Potters

'Singed by Fire', a 36 cm lustred wall plate featuring eucalyptus leaves

LUSTRE
for
China Painters and Potters

HEATHER TAILOR

Kangaroo Press

Acknowledgement
My gratitude is due to Helen Jones for her editorial skill
and encouragement.

Photography by Heather Tailor, John Austin and
Michael Goble-Garratt

Cover: 56 cm *'Strelitzia'* vase in orange, cinnamon, green, deep blue, yellow, ruby and silver-grey lustre

Reprinted 1991 and 1994
First published in 1990 by Kangaroo Press Pty Ltd
3 Whitehall Road Kenthurst NSW 2156 Australia
P.O. Box 6125 Dural Delivery Centre NSW 2158
Typeset by G.T. Setters Pty Limited
Printed in Hong Kong by Colorcraft Ltd

ISBN 0 86417 294 X

Contents

'Rainbow Bee-eaters', a 30 cm plate in lustre

Preface

During the last ten years I have been extremely fortunate in being able to teach lustre workshops in many other parts of Australia as well as in my own state of Western Australia.

Students at these seminars are often apprehensive about lustre work. Guiding them through the process of completing a piece and encouraging them to experiment with various techniques and different subjects has helped to promote their enthusiasm and confidence. As the workshops progress the students usually lose their inhibitions and become involved in the endless design possibilities that lustre work evokes.

Few china painting or pottery students have any formal art training, however; many feel unable to create designs of their own without the teacher's guidance. A good basic knowledge of the principles of design is essential for good results, no matter how creative or original the artist or craftsperson may be.

Art is a form of communication by which artists express their thoughts and feelings; each individual has something unique to contribute. With art education comes the ability to interpret these ideas and students must have the courage and confidence to study other art forms. There are many avenues of learning available in Australia—formal art courses for a certificate or diploma in art and design or, for the less committed, adult education or private drawing and design classes. Books on design, colour theory, art exhibition catalogues and other art forms also stimulate ideas.

With art experience and knowledge comes the potential for innovative work and the ability to explore new concepts that will possibly take china painting specifically from a decorative art to a fine art status.

Heather Tailor 1990

Introduction

I have been working and experimenting with commercial lustres on white porcelain for many years and more recently advising other potters on how to use them on their glazed pieces. This book, based on my experiences, gives beginners a starting point.

Before firing, most lustres appear to be brown fluids packaged in glass phials. Only their names give any indication of the fired colour. Testing and experimenting with each colour first is the only way to anticipate the final result.

Lustre is fast and easy to apply directly from the phial and can be rapidly fired to 720°C in a small electric kiln. Opening the kiln door is an exciting experience, as the fired result can be quite unpredictable, yet lustres can produce a range of soft subtle colours and fascinating iridescent rainbow effects.

This book is designed to guide painters through the basic techniques of working with lustres.

The artist's table, demonstrating various works in progress

1 What is Lustre?

The use of lustre is believed to have originated in Egypt about 800AD where it was used for glass decoration. From as early as the tenth century Islamic potters used shades of yellow, brown, green and red lustre over an opaque white tin glaze to decorate their wares. The technique spread to Spain, the town of Valencia becoming a major ceramic centre in the fifteenth century. The lustrewares of Manises (a district of Valencia) became famous throughout Europe.

The lustre techniques used by these early potters required a smoky reduction firing. Metallic salts and carbonates were mixed into a paste with red ochre and applied to a low fired (800°C) tin glaze. The ware was fired in an updraft kiln using oak for fuel. In the smoky atmosphere, the metallic oxides reduced to a thin metal film, fusing with the glaze between 600 and 700°C. For the lustre film to bond to the ware, it was essential for the glaze to begin melting at the temperature at which the lustre reduced to a film. When the ware was removed from the kiln, it was black from the smoke and had to be washed and polished to reveal the lustre design.

Today a large range of commercial lustres is available. These are called *oxidation lustres* because they are fired in an oxidising kiln, a kiln in which there is an ample supply of air. Electric kilns are oxidising kilns.

Commercial lustre is in liquid form and contains solutions of metallic salts, bismuth, resin and oils. Upon firing, the resin and oil burn out, releasing carbon which acts as the reducing agent. A very thin film of metal is deposited on the glazed surface and fluxed onto the glaze by the bismuth.

Various effects can be obtained by varying the thickness of the films or altering the consistency and concentration of the solution.

Lustres contain no glaze and are only as shiny as the glaze over which they are applied. Lustre is at its best on a glossy surface. It owes its beauty to reflected light, so that convex and concave surfaces display different effects.

Commercial lustres are available in many different colours. They can be transparent, opaque, light, dark or metallic, all having varying degrees of iridescence.

Fresh lustre should be quite liquid and easy to apply. Evaporation, heat and age cause lustre to thicken and eventually 'gel'. Some gel within months of manufacture, others stay in good condition for years. It is wise not to keep lustres too long; use them within a year, storing phials in the refrigerator in very hot weather. The glass phials should be full to the top to avoid evaporation into the air space.

When lustre is applied to a clean white glossy glazed surface and fired to between 720 and 750°C it forms a thin leaf one-100 000th of an inch thick. Unlike onglaze paint that will chip and blister when too many coats are applied, lustre can be applied in many layers without the risk of chipping. Each coat is fired before another is applied. Colours can be deepened by applying several fired coats. Some colours can be blended into one another.

The fluid lustre is very versatile and can be applied in a smooth, even layer, a dappled mottled layer or gradated from a light to heavy application. It can be applied by brush or sponge, and even 'floated' on. The tacky surface can be streaked with a stiff brush, imprinted by pressing on plastic wrap, cracked with marbelising liquid, haloed with solvent and dribbled with thinner.

Different colours can be fired over one another to produce many shades. Pearl can be applied over any fired lustre to produce iridescent lights. Transparent lustres can be applied over gold, platinum, bronze, copper and black to create unusual iridescent metallic colours.

The highly glazed finish of lustre is very susceptible to scratching, which means lustre should only be used on decorative pieces, not on articles for domestic use.

2 Hazards in using lustre

Lustre, thinner, solvents, masking lacquers and lustre resists are all **toxic substances**.

Strict hygiene principles should be observed. Paint in a well ventilated room and avoid breathing the fumes. Do not eat or smoke while painting and wash hands after use.

Brushes or cotton tips should not be licked.

Fumes from the kiln are also very toxic.

Materials for lustre work. Lustre, thinner, solvents and lustre resists are toxic substances

3 Surfaces to use

Lustre can be applied to any fired glazed ceramic surface as an onglaze technique. White porcelain, bone china, tiles, glazed ceramic and glass are all excellent surfaces.

Lustre is best applied over a high-fired glossy surface. The colours fire bright, clear and shiny and will take a firing of between 720 and 800°C.

Over semi-matt surfaces lustre fires less glossy and loses some of its reflective iridescence.

Over matt surfaces lustre will not glaze and loses all of its iridescence.

Lustre will produce slightly different colours over low-fired glazes such as bone china, tiles and some types of ceramic, because the glaze on these wares starts to soften at the lustre firing temperature. The firing temperature can therefore be lowered to between 680 and 720°C.

Lustre will fire on glass at 600°C. At this temperature, lustre is at its very minimum firing temperature and adheres to the glass because the surface is starting to soften. Never attempt to fire glass higher than 600°C, as beyond this temperature glass changes its molecular structure from a solid to a liquid and will slump.

As most coloured lustres are transparent, coloured glazes will show through. Lustre can be used to enhance a coloured glaze or alter it. A turquoise or pale blue lustre applied over a blue-grey glaze will deepen the colour. A pink, on the other hand, would change the colour of the glaze to more of a violet-grey.

Lustre fires transparent on glass—the iris design painted on the front and back of this 30 cm vase appears as one image

4 Drawing onto the surface

Unless you are very confident with freehand work, sketch a design onto the glaze before applying lustre. Any pen or pencil that you use must be easy to use, quick to remove and should fire out without harming the lustre.

Chinagraph pencils and watercolour pencils such as Aquarelles are ideal for marking out a design. Always use sparingly, leaving only faint lines.

Never use graphite pencils or carbon. These can leave lines under the lustre, especially under gold.

Chinagraph and Aquarelle pencils can be used to back a tracing for transfer to the surface to be worked. Trace the design from the pattern on tracing paper, using a ballpoint pen. Turn the tracing over and scribble the pencil over the back of it. Lay the tracing onto the surface and redraw with a ballpoint pen. The ballpoint will press the pencil onto the glaze, leaving fine lines.

A fine felt-tipped pen is also an ideal marker which fires out. I use an Artline 200 to sketch and explore design ideas on the ware. It moves quickly and smoothly over the surface and erases with a damp tissue.

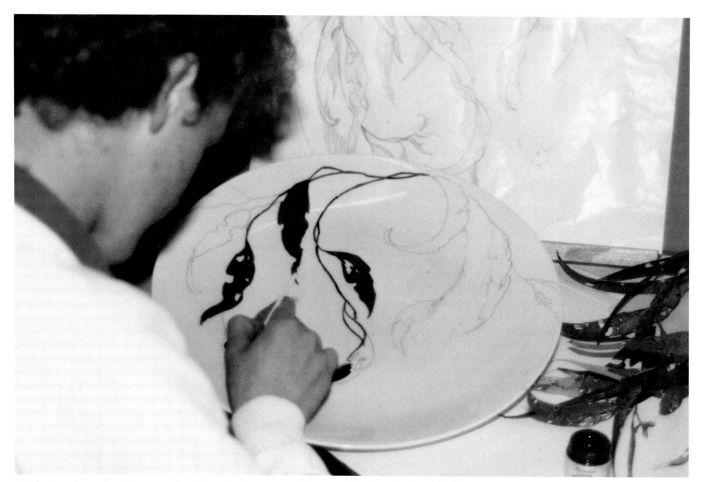

A felt tipped pen has been used to draw the leaves on this porcelain plate before blocking them in with lustre resist

5 Application

Lustres are applied direct from the phial onto a clean glazed surface. A clean surface is essential—any dust can spoil the finish by leaving spots in the colour. Wipe the surface with a tissue wet with methylated spirits before applying lustre.

Make sure the applicator is clean. Dirty brushes can transfer the dregs of other paints and colours into the lustre, leaving dirty streaks, dulling the sheen or greying the colour. Dirty pieces of sponge can transfer specks of dust; an old crumbling sponge can leave tiny bits of sponge stuck to the tacky layer, which melt in the firing to leave white spots.

On application, lustre will dry quickly, especially in a warm room. Be prepared to work quickly and use lustre or gold thinner to slow the drying time if necessary. Remember that thinner will dilute the colour and if it is not mixed into the lustre properly, or too much is used, it will leave white spots in the finish.

Lustre can be applied in a thin layer or more heavily, but there is a limit to how much lustre can be applied in one application. Some lustres blister, crack and dull if applied too thickly.

A smooth thin layer is preferable to a thick, patchy, heavy layer. The thin layer can be re-coated after firing and built up to the required depth of colour over several firings.

Always work quickly when applying lustre; avoid working in front of a heater or in moving air, which will dry the lustre faster than normal.

When applying lustre to large upright shapes, work in a broad panel from top to bottom, then work in both directions, working the lustre to the right, then to the left, back and forth until the coat merges. Do not neglect one edge and work around in one direction. This edge may be dry by the time you reach it.

Once lustre has dried, do not attempt to apply any more wet lustre over it. The lustre will become quite tacky before it dries, so once this stage is reached, it is best to stop and fire. Wet lustre applied over dried lustre lifts off parts of the dry coat so that the finish is patchy and uneven. Tiny pieces of sponge or hairs from the applicator can stick very easily to a roughened surface.

If the application is unsuccessful, wipe the lustre off with methylated spirits and start again.

Sponge

The easiest way to apply lustre is with a piece of sponge. The sponge leaves a slight stippled texture on the fired finish, varying with the grain of the sponge. Using a sponge is also the easiest way of covering large areas smoothly and quickly, of blending, gradating and lifting off excess lustre.

Sponge can be cut to any size to suit, and thrown away after use. Offcuts of foam sponge can be purchased from stores selling casual furniture and from upholstery factories. Compare the grain of the pieces available and choose the finest. I cut the sponge into small blocks with an electric knife (or scissors) and store it in plastic bags to keep out the dust.

To apply the lustre, I tear a small block of sponge in half, open it out and use the inside surface. This is a simple precaution against transferring any dust particles to the wet lustre. The other piece can be used for lifting off excess, and blending or fading out edges.

Another handy material is foam bandage, generally used for supporting sporting injuries, which is supplied in a roll of very fine thin sponge sheet. A small piece can be wrapped around a block of sponge or folded into a pad to apply the lustre. This bandage is so fine that it leaves very little texture in the finish.

Tailor the size of the sponge to the size of your piece—small pieces for small areas and a large block to cover larger areas.

The lustre can be tipped directly onto the sponge. Always wipe the sponge across the top of the phial to spread the lustre evenly across the sponge surface; do not tip the lustre on to one spot, otherwise it will soak down into the thirsty sponge which will imprint with blobs.

Direct application from the phial is ideal for small quickly covered areas. When a large surface is encountered, tip some lustre into a clean dish, add a few drops of thinner and blend thoroughly with a clean brush, then dip the sponge into the pool. Before applying, work the lustre across the sponge surface by sponging up and down on the dish, or by scraping it on the rim of the dish until it is loaded evenly.

For a smooth result, apply the lustre evenly and keep sponging back and forth over the surface until all the bubbles have gone and it appears even. The surface will start to 'ping', indicating the lustre is becoming tacky. This is very important for a smooth application because if the surface is left wet and blotchy, it will fire unevenly; as well, the wet surface attracts dust.

A dappled, mottled effect can be achieved by sponging the lustre on in thin and thick blobs, then allowing it to dry off naturally for a few minutes before sponging it dry.

To gradate lustre from a medium to heavy application to a very thin film, so that it fires dark to light, sponge on evenly, then lift some of the lustre off with a clean piece of sponge. This is also an excellent way of thinning lustre out when either too much has been applied or a very thin coat is required. I never pad lustre with silk. If I want a very light coat, I use this method.

Gradating lustre out so that it fades away to nothing is more difficult. It is very easy to get what I call a 'tide mark', where the lustre suddenly stops. One way to avoid this effect is to let the sponge gradually empty itself and at the same time reduce the pressure so that the outer edge only receives a very thin film of lustre. Another method is to sponge the lustre on, gradually letting the application diminish and applying less pressure, then using a clean piece of sponge, working back over the outer edge lifting excess lustre off. Thinner added to the lustre will help in the gradating process.

Compatible colours can be blended into one another with sponge. Use a different piece of sponge for each colour. Sponge in a band of the first colour, change sponge and lay a band of the next colour alongside, then work back and forth to blend the two bands together. This can be done with many bands of colour. A word of warning, however—incompatible colours can fire grey when they mix and overlap, or separate slightly. Make sure the colours will blend and the effect is acceptable before attempting this effect. Experiment first.

Another method of blending colour into colour is to sponge one colour all over then, with a clean piece of sponge, to apply another colour into the wet coat and work it in. This is most effective when applying a darker colour from the top, bottom or side of a piece and blending it in.

All this sounds very complicated, but only practice makes perfect. Try experimenting with these techniques on test tiles, the backs of unwanted china plates, or any other cheap plates or dishes, before you attack a valuable piece.

Brush

Brushstrokes leave streaks and variations in transparent lustre. As part of the design, these brushmarks can be very expressive, but very disappointing when not required.

Synthetic brushes (imitation sables) are ideal for applying lustre, as the synthetic hairs do not moult as readily as natural hair. The hairs are soft and springy and the brushes cost less than natural hair brushes.

Useful shapes and sizes:
Small pointers from size 0 to 4
Flat square shaders, ¼'', ½'', ¾'' upwards (6 mm, 12 mm, 25 mm).

Pointed brushes will produce designs in the 'painterly' manner. Flat shaders are ideal for blocking in backgrounds and solid areas.

Some texts advise keeping one brush for each coloured lustre. This can be confusing and expensive. I have about fifteen lustre brushes of all shapes and sizes in constant use. Immediately they have been used, they are rinsed clean in lustre solvent (or brush cleaner, toluene or methylated spirits), then stood upright—usually in my empty coffee cup—ready to go down to the kitchen for a wash. I squeeze detergent onto the draining board and rub the brushes vigorously back and forth in it, then swish them through quite hot clean water. While still wet, neaten the hairs back into shape and the brush is ready to go back into the lustre brush jar.

Before applying lustre with a brush, tip a little puddle of the lustre into one side of a clean dish. Put a little thinner

For a smooth result, apply lustre evenly and keep sponging back and forth over the surface. Thinner added to the lustre will help keep the lustre 'open'

14

Pink and grey galahs in lustre brushwork

on the other side. Use the thinner like a medium to slow the drying, thin the lustre and lubricate the brush.

One of the major problems with painting realistic subjects or designs is that wet lustre is hard to see, especially on non-white glazes. When applied the lustre is a very light brown colour, giving no indication of the fired result, so painting is almost blind. The only way I can overcome these problems is firstly, to limit each application to one colour at a time and fire between colours. Secondly, I imagine I am painting in sepia tones and so concentrate on the brushstrokes and the values, letting the colour look after itself.

Brushing-in backgrounds and large areas with transparent lustre is easier and more fun. Brushstrokes can produce movement in the form of swirls and streaks. Cross hatching, dabs and stipples give textured effects. As the lustre becomes tacky, pull the brush through again and again, to accentuate the direction of the strokes. Some lustres have a tendency to smooth out, especially on very smooth surfaces.

Opaque lustres, such as liquid bright gold, platinum, bronze, copper and black are solid opaque colours when applied with a brush. For the best results with metallic lustres, brush them on evenly. After firing they may still look streaky—most of the solid metallics need two fired coats.

Brush application—'Ring of Fire', lustre brushwork on a plate and an oil lamp

Penwork

Any steel mapping pen can be used to apply lustre. Clean the nib with methylated spirits before use, then dip straight into the liquid lustre and use it like an ink.

Some lustres are quite thin and have a tendency to spread on the shiny surface, making the lines twice the applied width. Compensate by using very fine nibs and less pressure. Opaque lustres such as gold and platinum do not spread as readily as the thinner, lighter lustres.

Liquid bright gold is the most useful of the group for penwork. A design can be drawn in with gold and fired. Other lustres can be applied within individual areas of the design and progressively fired. Lustre will fire over gold, turning it into iridescent metallic colours. Gold lines can also be used over fired lustre to outline or decorate, or even to camouflage disaster areas. The gold will fire to a rich bright gold over fired lustre.

'Rainbow Bee-eaters'. The design on this 14 cm vase was penned on with gold first, then lustre was applied and progressively fired.

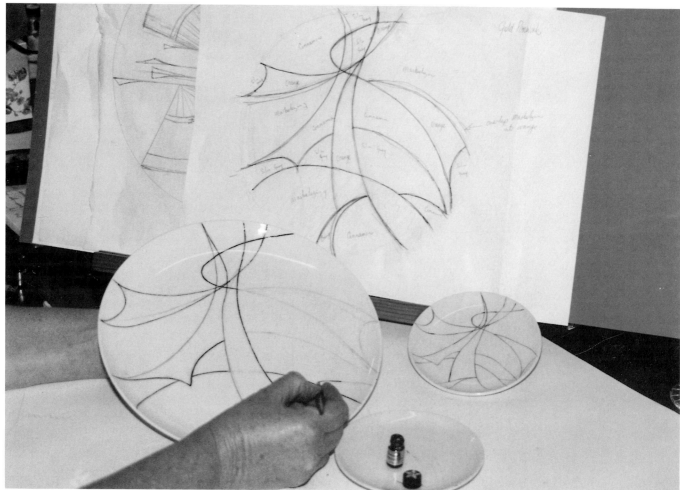

A design can be drawn in with gold and fired, then lustre can be applied to the individual areas

16

6 Firing

Lustres are fired in an electric or gas kiln. They will mature on a high fired glaze at 720°C and will take heat up to 800°C.

Lustre can be loaded into the kiln, even when not quite dry, and fired. Stilts can be used to separate porcelain as they will not mark dry lustre. Do not load heavily lustred pieces very close together; give them a little space to allow the air to circulate, otherwise the fumes may affect the surfaces.

A cylinder shape lustred right to the base should have a stilt placed under the base to lift it from the floor or kiln shelf, allowing the air to circulate during firing.

Leave the vents open in the kiln while firing.

I fire commercial white porcelain between 720 and 750°C.

On soft glazes, such as bone china, bathroom tiles and some soft ceramic glazes, firing should be between 680 and 720°C.

Glass is fired at 600°C.

When firing pieces smaller than 30cm in height or diameter, the kiln can proceed to 720°C in as little as one or two hours. I always switch my kilns onto high. My 33 cm kiln takes just over two hours to fire up to 720°C and my two small fast-firing kilns fire in under an hour when preheated. I paint and fire small pieces such as boxes and jewellery stones several times a day, cooling the kilns down quickly by opening the door a crack to release the heat. As the firing chambers are small, they quickly lose heat. I remove the pieces when they are still hot, but cool enough to handle with a cotton rag, and load another batch while the kiln is still warm. Larger pieces should be cooled more slowly.

Pieces over 30 cm and large ceramic tiles need a slower firing and slow cooling.

Glass can be fired fast, but it *must* be cooled slowly.

Lustres are fired to 720° in an electric or gas kiln

7 Lustre colours

Most of the lustre colours, whether very light, of medium density or dark colours, are transparent.

It is very important to test lustre colours before using them to find out how light and dark they fire. After firing one coat of lustre onto the glazed test pieces other coats can be applied and fired over the top.

Different colours can be fired over one another to create different hues. A fired pink lustre coated with a pale blue will fire a light violet. If the order is reversed and a fired pale blue lustre is coated with pink, the violet shade will be different. The colour applied last has the most effect on the colour combination.

A ruby or carmine lustre fires a medium density colour. If a blue lustre of similar tonal value is applied over the fired ruby, the result will be a rich violet. However, if the blue is darker than the ruby colour, the result will be a dark blue violet. When creating new colours by applying different coloured lustres over one another, try to use colours in the same value range for the best effects.

Because the last colour dominates the combination, light colours can be fired over each other and over the medium and darker colours. Medium colours can be used over dark colours, but dark colours can only be used as a base colour or over another dark lustre. Dark lustres block out any lighter colour lustre.

Colour groups

Lustre colours fall into four distinctive harmonising colour groups:

- Rose-pink—Carmine—Ruby—Red—Purple—Maroon—Violet
- Pale blue—Iridescent light blue—Turquoise—Dark blue
- Yellow-green—Green—Apple green—Dark green—Blue-green
- Yellow—Cinnamon—Orange—Light brown—Dark brown

The pink-violet group are very rich colours and the most expensive of all the transparent lustres. They also have the shortest shelf-life with a distinct tendency to gel if kept too long.

The blues fire slightly greyish, but they are very useful colours. Many shades of purple and violet can be made in combination with the pink and ruby coloured lustres. In combination with the greens, many blue-green shades can be made.

Good green lustres were quite elusive until recently. There are now several good clear greens on the market. In combination with yellow and cinnamon colours, shades such as chartreuse and olive-green can be made.

The yellows and oranges are very clear and bright, and are also the cheapest of the lustre colours. Orange fires particularly vivid; however, with brown overlaid it turns a rich autumn brown shade.

It is possible to blend some harmonising colours together on application, by sponging them alongside one another, then blending them into one another. Applying one colour, then working another colour over the top and blending, or brushing colours into one another, will result in effective blending. Sometimes a reaction occurs as one overlaps the other and it is advisable to experiment first with your lustre colours. Different brands of lustre can be safely used over one another.

Pink can be blended into ruby, ruby into violet, violet into dark blue and so on.

Yellow can be blended into cinnamon, cinnamon into orange and orange into light brown to create varied effects.

Light blue blends into turquoise, turquoise into dark blue, dark blue to ruby, red or violet.

Yellow blends into yellow-green, to green, to dark green to blue-green...

Never attempt to blend contrasting colours into one another as they can create a grey where they overlap.

I have successfully mixed colours together to create new shades, but again experiment first.

The next colour group includes the neutrals:

- Silver-grey—Blue-grey—Mother-of-pearl—Opal—White—Black

Silver-grey is very delicate and can be used to mute a vivid pink, ruby or red. The greys can also be used for shadows.

Mother-of-pearl and opal are transparent, highly iridescent lustres. Over a white glaze they result in a play of yellow, green, blue, pink and mauve lights. When used over other colours, they add an iridescent finish.

White is a clear lustre but when it is applied over another fired lustre it changes the colour slightly. White lustre makes green more vivid.

Black is almost opaque and usually classed as a metallic

lustre. Used thinly, black will fire a charcoal-grey and over a strong ruby-red turns dark maroon. Transparent lustres over black produce unusual colours, especially those with iridescence. Mother-of-pearl over fired black produces a black opal effect.

Testing lustres

Always test-fire lustres before using them. An ideal test piece is a white porcelain plate divided into segments like the spokes of a wheel. This can be done using sticky tape or masking tape.

Sponge or brush each segment with a lustre colour, let them dry and remove the tape. It is easier to do alternate segments in one firing and the other segments in a second firing, to avoid overlapping wet lustre. Add new lustres as your collection grows.

To realise the full potential of each colour, give part of each segment a second coat after the first firing, or even a third. Label them with gold penwork.

To test different lustre combinations, use tape to make bands across a test plate. Sponge each strip with a colour, peel off the tape and fire. Next firing, make bands across at right angles and sponge each colour on again in the same order. Remove the tape and fire again. Each colour will cross every other colour, creating many new colour combinations.

A white plate divided into segments makes an ideal test piece for lustre colours

Colour combinations—lustre over lustre

As there are many brands of lustre on the market, often with different names for the same colours, I have used common names to describe colour combinations in the list following. Most lustre types fire similarly and most of the combinations in the list should work with any brand.

Each lustre is fired separately. The combination can be reversed for a slightly different effect.

Pink over pale blue fires a mauve.
Ruby/carmine over turquoise-blue fires violet.
Ruby/carmine over dark blue fires deep blue-violet.
Ruby/carmine over violet fires purple.
Ruby/carmine over black fires maroon.
Pale blue over yellow-green fires jade-green.
Pale blue over light green fires water-green.
Pale blue over ruby/carmine fires violet.
Pale blue over yellow fires a greenish shade.
Turquoise-blue over green fires a blue-green.
Turquoise-blue over orange fires a dark iridescent green.
Turquoise-blue over copper fires metallic blue and violet.
Turquoise-blue over ruby/carmine fires blue-violet.
Green over black fires black-green.
Yellow over greens fire yellow-green shades.
Yellow over orange fires tangerine.
Yellow over turquoise-blue fires a greenish shade.
Orange over light brown fires burnt orange.
Light brown and dark brown over orange fires chestnut.
Cinnamon over mother-of-pearl fires a golden pearl.
Silver-grey over pink fires a soft dull violet.
Silver-grey or blue-grey over ruby/carmine fires violet.
Mother-of-pearl over pink fires pink pearl.
Mother-of-pearl over silver-grey fires grey pearl.
Mother-of-pearl over green fires green pearl.
Mother-of-pearl over black fires black opal.
Mother-of-pearl over gold fires iridescent gold.
Black over two coats of red fires maroon.

EXPERIMENT!

8 Stencilling

Stencilling with lustre creates limitless design possibilities. Several stencil techniques can be used—masking lacquers; self-adhesive tape, labels, plastic tape, masking tape and adhesive book cover; damp paper and lustre resists.

Masking lacquers

Waterbased Covercoat is a bright pink masking fluid for ceramics. It is designed to coat that part of the glaze that is not to be painted. It should not be used on unglazed areas.

Using the Covercoat, paint on a design with a brush (the brush can be washed in soap and water after use). When the Covercoat is quite dry it will stay in place while a lustre is applied.

When the lustre is tacky, carefully peel off the dry Covercoat. Do not fire the ware with any masking lacquer left on.

Spirit-based masking lacquers are also available, but do *not* use these for lustre. The wet lustre can react with this type of lacquer, making it sticky and difficult to peel off.

Adhesive tape

Self-adhesive tape and labels can be used to cover parts of the surface not to be lustred. Tape can be used to create bands, panels and borders. Geometric shapes can be created by taping around the outside of squares, triangles, oblongs, bands or any faceted shape.

Self-adhesive Contact and adhesive bookcover can be cut into any shape; labels of all shapes and sizes can be used to make blocks, circles, crescents or even stars. Labels can be applied separately or overlapping in continuous bands across the surface. Make sure tape or labels can be easily peeled off after the lustre has been applied. Allow the tape to overlap the edge of the porcelain piece so that the ends can be lifted off when the stencilling process is complete.

Newsprint, photocopy paper, butcher's paper or any absorbent paper can be sponged with water until damp but not dripping wet. The damp paper can be pressed onto the surface; it will hold there for a few minutes while lustre is applied. Landscape contours can be torn out of lengths of paper and successive bands of lustre sponged over to create lines of hills.

Another method is to cut out shapes that can be repeated. Sponge over each one, then lift the shape off and move to another location to create multiple images.

Lustre resists

Lustre resists are products specifically for lustre work; they must *not* be used for any other onglaze paint technique.

There are three types of lustre resists on the market. One, pale green or pale blue in colour, is called Resist-a-dec. The second is black and called Lustre Resist No. 3. Lastly there is White Pelikan Plaka, a thick cassein poster paint.

Lustre resists are painted on to block out a design area and allowed to dry. Unlike masking lacquers, which are thick and sticky to apply, resists resemble thick poster paint and can be diluted with water. Very detailed fine designs can be stencilled on by using fine-pointed brushes and pens. Resist can also be used to block around shapes.

Lustre resist cannot be peeled off. After the lustre has been applied, the resist stays on the surface and fires with the lustre in the kiln. Only after firing can the resist be rubbed off, leaving a stencilled shape.

Resist-a-dec, the pale blue and green resists, can only be used once. After firing they go powdery and rub off very easily. If another coat of lustre is required over the same design, these resists must be either removed and re-applied, or recoated to seal, otherwise they will lift off as the lustre is applied.

Lustre Resist No. 3 stays intact after firing. It does not go powdery and needs stronger rubbing to remove it after firing; another coat of lustre can be applied over it without damaging the original design. I use Lustre Resist No. 3 for most of my lustre work.

White Pelikan Plaka will also stay intact after firing and another coat of lustre can be applied over it without damaging the design. Black Pelikan Plaka may also be used, but it will go powdery and rub off after the first firing.

Stencilling—tape can be used to create bands for a geometric design

Lustred geometric boxes

9 Lustre resist work

This chapter describes how to use a lustre resist to create various designs. A few hints on how to apply and remove it easily may be helpful.

Try sketching the design with the resist, using a small pointed brush

Apply the resist heavily to completely block out the intended design area

Lustre Resist application

- Use Lustre Resist No. 3 or White Pelikan Plaka poster paint.
- Apply straight from the jar with a clean brush or a pen.
- Unwanted design can be removed with water and design areas tidied with damp cotton tips.
- Brush come clean in water.
- Water can be used to dilute these lustre resists if they become too thick or if a thinner solution is required to 'sketch' a design on the surface first. Too much water in the resist can cause it to flake after firing.
- Resist will not cover a greasy or waxy surface, so clean the surface first with methylated spirits. If the surface remains waxy, rub with a little Jif or other cream cleanser.
- Avoid drawing the design first with wax pencil. Unless tracing is imperative, try sketching the design with the resist itself with a small pointed brush or a felt-tipped pen.
- Apply the resist heavily to completely block out the intended design area. Check for thin areas and tiny gaps in the dry coat. Fill these in, otherwise the lustre will penetrate.

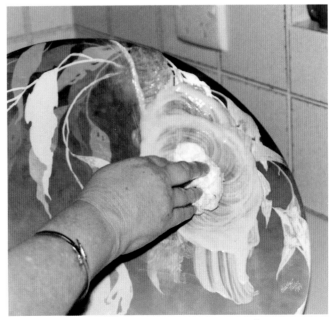

Removing resist after multiple firing with a non-abrasive cleaner which will not damage the fired lustre

- Use the appropriate sized brush: No. 0 or No. 1 pointed sable or synthetic brushes for outlining, miniature work and thin lines; larger brushes for blocking; mapping pens for fine lines, lettering, numbers, calligraphy, filigree and signatures.
- Remove any smears of resist from the surface with a damp tissue. Remove any pencil, tracing or finger marks and dust by wiping gently with methylated spirits. Methylated spirits will not move the dry resist unless pressure is used.
- Apply the lustre all over the piece. The resist will stop the lustre penetrating to the underneath layer.

Firing

- Over high-fired glazes, such as white porcelain, fire at 720°C to 750°C—no higher.
- Over low-fired glazes such as tiles, bone china and some ceramics, fire between 680°C and 700°C.

After firing

- The resist fires white or takes on the colour of the last coat of lustre applied.
- The fired resist will stay intact until you rub it off. Another coat of lustre can be applied over the resist immediately and refired.
- Always check the fired resist for areas that may be flaking off. Patch these up with fresh resist, but do not recoat any sound areas.

Stencilling onto fired lustre

- Lustre resist can be applied over any fired lustre and gold.
- The resist can be used to stencil shapes into the lustre background.
- Apply another coat of lustre over the original and new resist work and fire.
- Never over-fire lustre resist work. Over 750°C the resist can stick to the ware, dulling the lustre underneath and making it difficult to remove.
- Many fired coats of lustre can be applied onto the surface. Lustre resist can be used to stencil into them, so that each colour or value is preserved in the final design.

- A coat of resist becomes harder to remove as each successive coat of lustre is applied and fired over it. Five coats of lustre is about the maximum over resist.

Removing resist after multiple firings

- After one or two firings the resist will still clean off with methylated spirits.
- Resist that is difficult to remove can be cleaned off with cream cleanser or Jif (a non-abrasive cleaner for kitchen and bathroom use). Take the piece to the kitchen sink, squeeze the Jif all over the surface and rub clean. This non-abrasive cleaner will not scratch or damage the fired lustre.
- Do not use abrasive pads or abrasive cleaners such as Ajax—they will scratch.
- A gold eraser can be used to rub off unwanted spots of fired lustre; it will rub back to the glaze, however.

Using lustre resist makes possible the creation of quite complicated designs. In effect it is similar to some printmaking techniques. The parts covered by the resist will remain the colour of the original surface. As lustre is transparent, each successive fired coat makes the surface darker. The lightest colour is used first, the darkest last.

Applying a lustre resist design onto a white glaze and firing pink lustre over brings the piece out of the kiln pink. The original resist is left intact and more design is applied with resist to some of the pink areas. A pale blue lustre is applied and the piece fired again. The piece comes out of the kiln a light violet shade. Again the original coats of resist are left intact and more design added with fresh resist. Green lustre is applied and fired over; the piece comes out of the kiln an unusual blue-grey. Further stencilling is applied over the blue-grey, then a stronger coloured lustre such as a ruby or red is fired over for the last time. The piece comes out of the kiln a purple shade. When all the resist is cleaned off, there will be areas of white design, pink, violet and blue-grey on a dark background. The white shapes will be the most prominent area of the design.

The white areas can be left white or coloured in with lustre brushwork or gold penwork and refired to lustre temperature. They can be painted with an onglaze paint, iridescent metallic or a relief, such as raised paste, enamel or texture coat and fired to 800°C.

There are many possibilities to this technique. In chapter 11, Eucalyptus Leaves, I will demonstrate how to create a finished piece.

10 Special effects

Lustre can be diluted with thinner, dispersed with solvent and crackled with marbelising fluid. Lustre will float on top of water and form a skin which can be transferred to the glazed surface of a ceramic piece by a simple process called dipping. These techniques give random effects and the fired result can often be unpredictable. However, these informal applications can produce interesting combinations of colour, line and textural effects in the lustre.

Marbelising

A marbelising fluid is applied *over* an *unfired* coat of lustre or gold. The fluid cracks and splits the lustre film into an uneven honeycomb pattern during firing.

Every lustre colour marbelises differently and some marbelising fluids are more aggressive than others.

The lustre to be marbelised is applied to the ware with either a brush or sponge in a medium to heavy coat. The lustre is then left to dry at room temperature; some lustres dry in a few minutes, while others may take several hours. The best time to marbelise is when the lustre is just dry to touch. The marbelising fluid is painted over the lustre with a large soft brush in one single application. Do not rework, and avoid overlapping strokes. The piece is left to dry, then fired to 720°C.

After firing the surface should be cleaned with a damp cloth to remove any residue. The marbelising brush can be cleaned in soap and water immediately after use.

Many factors govern the degree of success with this technique. If the lustre is too dry, the marbelising fluid cannot split and crack the surface. If the lustre is too wet, the marbelising brush will lift off some of the lustre and spoil the finish.

Never use heat to force-dry the lustre, as the ceramic body heats up and dries the lustre from the back, making the marbelising action impossible. Moving air is more successful in speeding up the drying time.

The thickness of the layer of lustre to be marbelised is also important. Thin layers dry quickly but do not marbelise as successfully as a medium to heavy layer.

The amount of marbelising fluid used over the lustre can also affect the result. A very thin layer will not marbelise as aggressively as a medium to heavy application. Excess marbelising fluid will remove the lustre, often a problem when brush strokes overlap. Never sponge marbeliser on as the sponge can lift off areas of lustre.

Lustre resist may be used as a stencilling fluid in conjunction with marbelising effects. The marbeliser will not harm lustre resist or mark unpainted areas of glaze or any fired lustre or paint work. Any fluid that overlaps onto other parts of the ware will fire away in the kiln.

Marbelising gives the best results over a white or light-coloured highly glazed surface. The fine network of marbelised lines shows up in strong contrast. Semi-matt surfaces or matt do not marbelise successfully.

Copper lustre marbelises very effectively and is a good lustre with which to begin. It dries quickly and the dark colour over a white surface shows up the intricate marbelised pattern. Liquid bright gold and platinum are also recommended for marbelising.

Marbelising with white lustre

Another technique is to marbelise a layer of white lustre first and apply a coloured lustre over. This technique gives different results, usually producing a wider spaced honeycomb effect.

White lustre is painted over the area to be marbelised. When just dry, the marbelising fluid is applied over the white lustre and left to dry thoroughly. A coat of coloured lustre or one of the metallic lustres is applied over the area. When dry, fire the piece to 720°C.

Running and dribbling

Gold and lustre thinner, which is generally used for diluting and slowing the drying time of lustre, are used for the technique of running and dribbling. Select an upright shape and coat the entire piece with thinner. Using a clean brush for each colour, touch or wipe brushfuls of lustre onto the wet surface and allow it to run down. If necessary, mix thinner with the thicker lustres.

The lustre dribbles will run slowly down the surface; it is advisable to allow each colour a few minutes to make a pattern before applying more or the next colour. The lustre usually runs into snaking lines that divide and branch. The effect is reminiscent of trees and undergrowth, even coral and seaweed.

For the best results use harmonious colours or lustre colours that will blend. Contrasting colours, when used together wet, will merge in some areas as they dribble and fire grey. Contrasting colours are best applied in separate firings.

Lustre resist can be used to stencil designs in combination with running and dribbling with thinner. Trees can be stencilled onto a surface with lustre resist, the piece coated with thinner and dribbled with lustres and fired. The lustre effect will look like a forest backdrop with white stencilled trees. Details on the trees could be painted with onglaze paints, enamels and lustres, or penned in gold. Weeds, grasses and wheat are other suggestions suitable for this technique.

Lustres can be dribbled across two-dimensional surfaces to create abstract designs. Running lustres in bands across a tile or plate can create landscape effects.

Dribbled lustre can be confined to specific areas of a design by using either lustre resist or a masking lacquer to cover the other areas.

Dribbling often results in a build-up of excess lustre and thinner at the bottom of the piece; these areas can blister in the kiln. It is advisable to carefully lift off any excess lustre with a clean brush or blot the area with a tissue.

Methylated spirit will completely remove any unwanted areas of lustre and thinner.

Dispersing and halos

Solvent will immediately dilute lustre. If it is splashed, sprayed or dropped onto tacky lustre, holes will open up in the lustre film.

Lustre brush cleaner, dispersing agent, acetone, methylated spirits, toluene and spirits of turpentine as well as many other paint solvents will make spots of various sizes in wet lustre.

For controlled dispersing, use a small pointed brush dipped into a lustre solvent to apply tiny drops to tacky

Experiments with marbelising, mother-of-pearl, and mixing wet lustres together

'Pink and Platinum Leaves'—a 35 cm plate showing marbelising

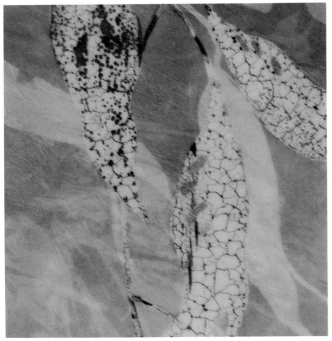

Special effects—marbelising fluid has split the platinum into a random honeycomb pattern during firing

lustre. The solvent will disperse the lustre outward, forming a hole with a ring of thicker lustre around the outside, hence the name 'halo'.

A toothbrush can be used to flick solvent onto wet lustre for random effects.

Solvents dry quickly and the holes in tacky lustre will stay crisp. However, if the lustre has been applied heavily and is too wet, the holes can close over before firing. Dry lustre is difficult to halo as the solvent does not penetrate. Always work with tacky lustre to create halos.

For random effects, lustre can be mixed with solvent and splashed on. Puddles and blobs will spread outward and dry rapidly.

Multiple halo effects can be created by making a large halo in the lustre, then touching smaller drops into the centre to create smaller and smaller rings. Different coloured diluted lustres can also be used.

Halos can be made in one coat of lustre and the piece fired to 720°C. Another coloured lustre can be applied and halos dispersed into the tacky coat, the piece being fired once again. The halos will show through the transparent layers.

Three vases titled 'Hang Down', 'Hang About' and 'Hang On' feature porcelain medallions fired onto their sides

Detail of one of the medallions showing the halos in the lustre

Dipping

Lustre floats on water and forms a skin which can be transferred to a surface by dipping a piece into the water. Compatible colours can be floated together for multicoloured effects.

Use a disposable plastic container for the water bath and use warm water to make the lustre form a skin more quickly. Choose a piece to dip that is convex in shape rather than concave—ball shapes are ideal. Make sure the water container is large enough to take the piece without the water spilling over the side when the piece is dipped into it.

With the lustre phial close to the water, tip a few drops onto the surface. The lustre will immediately spread out over the surface. Different colours can be dropped in together; each will react differently on the water surface. Some stay as blobs and have to be coaxed to spread out; others are so heavy they drop to the bottom. Experiment to find colours which give the best results.

When the lustre has formed a skin on the surface, gently dip the piece into the water and pick up the floating lustre. It is advisable to wear disposable plastic gloves while dipping. Methylated spirits will clean away excess lustre.

Allow the piece to dry before firing at 720°C.

Lustre resist and water-based masking lacquers cannot be used in conjunction with dipping; the water dilutes waterbased stencilling fluids, so a spirit-based masking lacquer should be used if you wish to combine dipped work with other techniques.

Other surface effects

The wet unfired surface of lustre is very vulnerable. Dust will mark the fired lustre; finger marks will show if the piece is handled while tacky and the lustre will lift off if the wet areas come into contact with another surface.

Plastic food wrap can be pressed onto the wet lustre and peeled off, lifting off some of the lustre and leaving unusual wrinkled effects.

Experiment by pressing other materials onto the wet surface; leaves, net, foil and fabric, for example, all give interesting effects.

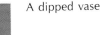

A dipped vase

Plastic food wrap can be pressed onto wet lustre and peeled off to leave an unusual wrinkled effect

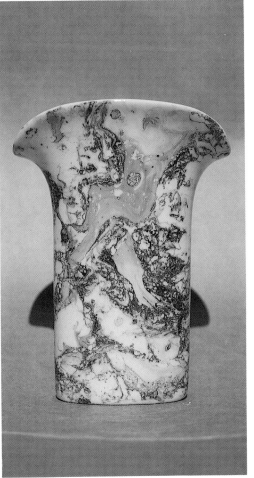

11 Eucalyptus leaves

The steps in working this vase are described on pages 32 and 33.

Paint the leaves in solid lustre resist

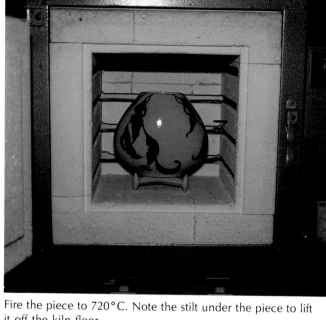

Fire the piece to 720°C. Note the stilt under the piece to lift it off the kiln floor

Applying the cinnamon and orange lustre

After the first firing

Paint in new leaves and stems with lustre resist and apply light brown and dark brown lustre

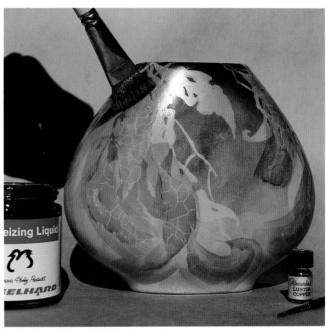

Marbelising the copper lustre leaves

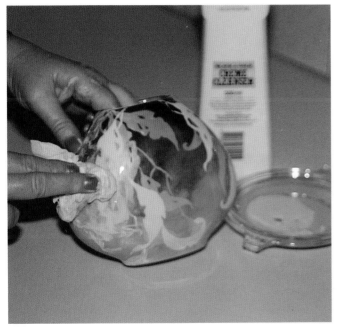

Removing the resist with cream cleanser

'Eucalyptus Leaves'—the finished piece

Inspiration

After a bushfire the singed gum leaves that have survived the flames curl and twist. They turn shades of russet, chestnut and deep orange with smokey black tinges. The colours and textures are reminiscent of orange, cinnamon, light brown and marbelised copper lustre. The pictures on the two previous pages show the development of a leaf design.

Materials

- White porcelain vase
- Lustre Resist No. 3 and a jar of water
- Small pointed brush to apply resist
- Several small blocks of foam sponge
- Two small clean dishes
- Marbelising fluid (optional)
- Cinnamon, orange, light brown and dark brown lustres (copper optional)

First stage

Using lustre resist on the tip of a small pointed brush, sketch the leaves and stems onto the porcelain. Do not overlap any of the leaves. Make the leaf shapes interesting! Australian gum leaves are often tattered and worm-holed.

The sketch can easily be corrected by removing the lustre resist with a damp tissue or cotton tip.

When the layout is complete, paint the leaves in solid lustre resist so that none of the surface is visible (except the wormholes, of course).

After the resist has dried, gently wipe the entire piece with a soft tissue and methylated spirits to remove any smears, grease and dust. Methylated spirits will not remove dry unfired lustre resist unless excess pressure is applied.

Tip a quantity of cinnamon lustre into one of the clean dishes and orange lustre into the other. Dip a small block of sponge into the cinnamon. Apply the cinnamon lustre to about half the surface and sponge until even. Dip a clean piece of sponge into the orange lustre and apply to the remaining areas of the piece. Overlap the orange into the wet cinnamon about 20 to 30 mm and sponge back and forth blending the two lustres together. Sponge the orange until even. Discard the blocks of sponge and return any unused lustre to its respective phials.

Fire the piece to 720°C.

When the piece comes out of the kiln the lustre resist leaves will be almost white in colour. (The black stain in Lustre Resist No. 3 is only a colouring agent which fires out leaving the resist white or tinted by whatever lustre colour has been applied.)

If the fired lustre colours are too light or patchy, another coat of lustre can be applied immediately to deepen the shade and fired before going on to the next step.

Second stage

Leaving the original leaf design intact, sketch in another spray of leaves, overlapping and interlacing through the first design. These leaves will be orange and cinnamon. Paint in the new leaves and stems with solid lustre resist and allow to dry.

Tip a quantity of light brown lustre into a clean dish and, using a clean block of sponge, apply the lustre to the entire piece. Sponge until even. Use a clean piece of sponge to lift off some of the light brown where it crosses the lighter coloured cinnamon lustre. While the lustre is still wet a small amount of dark brown lustre can be applied over the light brown to create a darker edge or a focal area in the design.

Fire the piece to 720°C.

The piece can be recoated with lustre and fired again if necessary.

Third stage

Remove all the lustre resist by using a tissue dipped in either methylated spirits or cream cleanser to rub the resist off. The original leaves will be white, with orange and cinnamon leaves behind. The background will be a chestnut-brown shade.

There are several options for finishing off the white leaves:

- Paint naturalistically with onglaze paints and fire to 800°C.
- Paint with raised paste or texture coat and fire to 800°C. After firing, coat with gold or copper and refire to 720°C.
- Penwork the leaves in gold or copper lustre.
- Paint or ground with metallic iridescent paints.
- Marbelise with copper lustre, as below.

Marbelising the leaves

Paint each white leaf and stem with copper lustre. Use a small synthetic pointed brush and apply the copper heavily. Allow the copper lustre to dry naturally, testing with your finger tip until the surface is tacky but the lustre does not lift off when touched.

Dip a large soft brush into marbelising fluid and apply over the copper-lustred leaves and stems in *one stroke*. Do not overlap or rework. Allow to dry and fire to 720°C.

Colour variation

Paint the leaf design in rose and silver-grey lustre with marbelised platinum leaves (see illustration on page 27).

Substitute the cinnamon and orange with rose lustre in the first stage. While the rose lustre is still wet, press plastic wrap onto the surface and peel off, leaving a textured effect in the tacky lustre.

Substitute the light brown and dark brown lustre with silver-grey in the second stage.

After the lustre resist has been cleaned off in the third stage, coat the white leaves with platinum and marbelise.

33

12 Dragonfly box

Inspiration

Dragonflies have intricate wing designs and are an ideal subject for lustre resist penwork. Lustre is also an ideal medium to depict their iridescent wings and bodies.

Materials

- Porcelain box
- Lustre Resist No. 3 and jar of water
- Mapping pen
- Copper, green and turquoise lustres
- Lustre brush
- Small block of sponge
- A dispersing agent (see section on special effects, page 26)

First stage

Sketch or trace the dragonfly onto the box lid using a non-greasy pencil or a fine felt pen.

Dip the mapping pen into the lustre resist and pen in the outline of the dragonfly's wings and tail. Fill in the fine details of the wing structure. Cross-hatch the eyes and draw in the legs. Block out the tail and body in solid resist. If the lustre resist is thick, dilute with a little water for penwork.

When the resist is dry, sponge copper lustre over the entire piece. Lift some of the wet copper off with a clean piece of sponge across one corner. (Copper lustre will fire an attractive violet colour when applied very thinly, so by lifting some of the copper off, the lustre will fire a rich copper graduating into a violet shade.)

Fire the piece to 720°C.

Second stage

Leave the lustre resist dragonfly intact.

Sponge turquoise-blue and green lustre unevenly over the piece. Lift some of the lustre off with a clean piece of sponge leaving only a very thin film in some areas.

When the lustre is tacky, make random halos by touching drops of solvent onto the surface (see special effects section, page 26).

Fire to 720°C.

Third stage

Remove the resist with a tissue dipped in methylated spirits or cream cleanser.

The dragonfly's wings, body and tail will be white. Using a small lustre brush, paint the tail and body in green, blue or yellow lustre. Paint the eyes in yellow or light brown lustre.

Fire to 720°C.

Enamel and gold can be used as further options to accent the design.

Dragonfly box, first stage. With lustre resist pen in the wings of the dragonfly and block out the tail and body

Making halos with solvent

Finished dragonfly box—in copper lustre haloed with green and turquoise

Dribbling and running lustre with thinner

Finished ruby and turquoise lustre ball vase

'Orange Poppies'—first stage. Paint the poppies with orange lustre. The unfired lustre is a light brown colour

Detail of the lustre brushwork on the orange poppies before firing

Second stage—'Orange Poppies' after the first firing

Finished piece—silver-grey lustre shadow shapes have been added to the background to finish the piece

15 Coping with disappointing results

Disasters do happen in lustre work. Most of them are due to lack of experience with the material.

Experimenting with the lustre colours, making test pieces, keeping notes and planning a design based on the results will contribute to successful pieces. Even then, something can go wrong because mistakes are not always obvious until the piece is fired.

The wrong colour can be used accidentally as all lustres appear a similar colour until fired. Labelling the lids of the lustre phials with coloured spots helps prevent this problem.

Dirty brushes can leave grey marks in lustre brushwork.

Lustre applied too thickly will blister and dull the surface; dust and grease will spoil the fired finish.

One of the most common problems is that the lustre fires too dark.

The question I am most frequently asked when a disaster occurs is, 'What will I do with it now?'

Here are some tips to help overcome some of the pitfalls.

Removing fired lustre

Acid is the only substance that will remove fired lustre. Rustiban (available from pharmacies), a product for removing rust from carpets and fabrics, contains 10% hydrofluoric acid which will strip fired lustre off the ceramic surface very quickly.

Hydrofluoric acid is a very dangerous corrosive acid that can eat into the skin and inflict painful damage to flesh and bone. The fumes can burn the eyes, throat and lungs. Seek immediate medical assistance if a burn occurs.

It is essential that sensible safety precautions are taken when using Rustiban—wear rubber gloves, cover the work area with newspaper or a sheet of plastic, and have a bucket of water ready to neutralise the acid.

Rustiban will remove *all* the fired lustre back to the white surface; it cannot be used to lighten a fired lustre colour.

To remove lustre from the surface with acid, lay a tissue over the lustre; carefully shake drops of Rustiban onto the tissue until it is soaked and clinging to the surface. Allow the acid to work for two or three minutes and then rub the surface with the soaked tissues to remove the lustre. (The tissues hold the acid in contact with the surface and stop it drying.) *The acid should be left on only long enough for easy removal of the fired lustre as it will continue to corrode the surface and dull the glaze if it is not neutralised.*

When all the lustre is removed, neutralise the acid by washing the surface thoroughly in water. Dispose of the acid-soaked tissues and paper sensibly and wash the rubber gloves.

A small section of a lustred design can be removed by dipping a cotton tip into Rustiban and rubbing the area until the lustre dissolves. Neutralise with water immediately.

Rustiban can also be used to stencil a white shape into a lustred area. Surround the shape with a wide band of spirit-based masking lacquer and allow to dry. Gently rub the area to be removed with a cotton tip soaked in Rustiban; for larger stencilled shapes, use tissues. Neutralise the acid with water and peel off the masking lacquer.

Covering lustre mistakes

Fired lustre can be darkened by adding another coat of lustre and refiring. Uneven lustre, tide marks, dust and unwanted speckles can usually be covered or camouflaged with another coat of colour.

Fired dark lustre cannot be lightened, although it is tempting to try and mute the colour by applying a lighter hue over it and refiring. Mother-of-pearl will add an iridescent play of coloured lights to a dark lustre and give the illusion of a lighter surface.

A lustred design can be completely obliterated by firing coats of lustre over until the original image has disappeared. Different colours can be sponged over and blended to create unusual hues. The piece can then be reworked with another design using the lustre as a background.

Relief materials such as Texture Coat, enamels and raised pastes can be applied over fired lustre. The *fired* texture can be covered with liquid bright gold, copper, bronze or platinum.

Transparent lustres will colour any white relief surface.

Fire all relief paint to 800°C.

Fire gold, copper, bronze and lustre colours over fired relief paint to 700°C.

Fire platinum over fired relief paint to 680°C.

Liquid bright gold is completely opaque and will effectively cover lustre.

Gold penwork can be used to outline and draw a design over fired lustre. Implied texture in gold penwork, such as cornelli work, dots, pebbles and scales can be used to pattern the surface.

Gold, copper, bronze and platinum can be applied and marbelised over fired lustre.

Larger solid areas of fired gold and copper can be lustred and turned into iridescent metallic colours.

Some of the best pieces are reworked disasters!

A reworked vase. The original design has been removed and relief materials have been applied

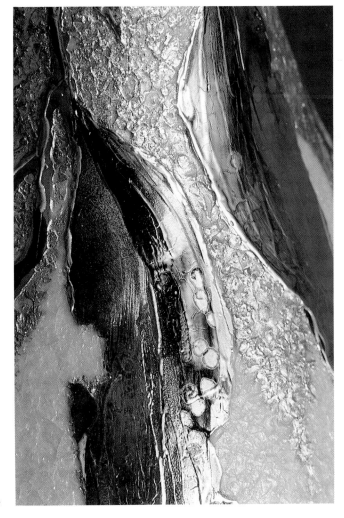

Detail showing the fired texture covered with gold and lustre

16 Showcase

56 cm *'Strelitzia'* vase in orange, cinnamon, green, deep blue, yellow, ruby and silver-grey lustre

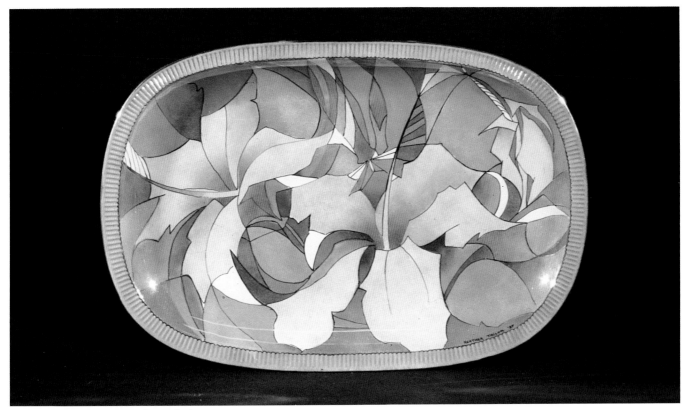

'Abstract Hibiscus'—30 cm lustred platter

'Pelicans'

'Magpies'—30 cm wall plate in black lustre

Lustred jewellery

Teapot in lustre

Lustred jewellery

'Desert Peas'—35 cm lustred plate

'Strelitzia ravenala' in lustre, platinum, gold and copper marbelising over Texture Coat relief.
The Texture Coat has created semi-matt surfaces within the design which produce different
colours and less gloss

Index